Death by Petticoat

American History
Myths Debunked

Mary Miley Theobald

with The Colonial Williamsburg Foundation

Andrews McMeel
Publishing®

a division of Andrews McMeel Universal

Andrews McMeel Publishing
a division of Andrews McMeel Universal
1130 Walnut Street, Kansas City, Missouri 64106

www.andrewsmcmeel.com

The Colonial Williamsburg Foundation
www.history.org

16 17 18 19 20 TEN 10 9 8 7 6

ISBN: 978-1-4494-1853-3

Library of Congress Control Number: 2011944561

Attention: Schools and Businesses

Andrews McMeel books are available at quantity discounts with bulk purchase for educational, business, or sales promotional use. For information, please e-mail the Andrews McMeel Publishing Special Sales Department: specialsales@amuniversal.com.

Other Colonial Williamsburg books by Mary Miley Theobald

Williamsburg Christmas (with Libbey Hodges Oliver)

Colonial Williamsburg: The First 75 Years

Recipes from the Raleigh Tavern Bakery

Contents

Preface

Every day, stories that are not true are repeated in museums, national parks, and historic sites and on bus tours and walking tours. Some are outright fabrications. Others contain a kernel of truth that has been embellished over the years. Because they are catchy, humorous, or shocking, these stories often stick in our memories when quieter information slips away.

History myths are not history mistakes. They usually seek to explain something, such as why kitchens in the South were separate from the main house (Myth #21). Some are based on mistakes or erroneous beliefs, such as Myth #17 (the Dutch bought Manhattan from the Indians for $24 worth of beads) or Myth #18 (the Good Friday Massacre of 1622 took place on Good Friday). Others make us feel superior, such as Myth #54 (people didn't bathe back then), or tease our interest in secrets and codes, as does Myth #45 (the position of a horse's legs on an equestrian statue tells how the rider died).

How do myths get started? Usually there is a kernel of truth that has been exaggerated, as in Myth #19 (most men wore wigs in colonial America), or taken out of context, as in Myth #46 (it was against the law to teach African-Americans, slave or free, to read). Sometimes we apply today's logic to yesterday, as in Myth #6 (when men smoked tobacco, they often shared clay pipes; for sanitary reasons, they would break off the tip of the stem before passing the pipe). Or we apply something that was true at one time or place to another time or place when it was not, as in Myth #3 (since most early Americans were illiterate, shops signs had to use pictures instead of words).

How do myths spread? Any museum docent or tour guide will tell you that visitors bring them up, having heard them at other sites or from other people. They can spread from docent to docent as new people repeat what the older ones are saying. They are most common in museums where training and supervision are poor, and on bus tours, carriage tours, ghost tours, and walking tours where the emphasis is on entertainment, not education. In such instances, any story that is funny, scary, shocking, or sexy will be repeated endlessly, even when the guides know it isn't true. Sadly, many myths are spread through flawed textbooks: One fifth-grade Virginia textbook was recently withdrawn when it was discovered to contain dozens of errors and myths, such as "very few people in colonial America could read" (Myth #3) and "every single American died at the Alamo" (Myth #52).

It is hard to visit a historic site or museum today without encountering at least one of these myths. How many have you heard? How many do you believe?

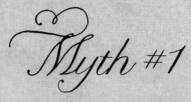

Myth #1

So many colonial American women died from
burns when their long petticoats caught fire
that it became the second–most common
cause of death, after childbirth.

*B*urning to death sounds gruesome, and there *were* some instances in which women died of burns when their long skirts, or petticoats, came too close to hearth fires.

But historians who have studied death records from the first couple centuries of American history have determined that the leading cause of death for women was neither childbirth nor burns; it was *disease*. The Death by Petticoat myth is a huge exaggeration. How did it come about? Perhaps the horrific nature of these rare accidents made them stick in people's minds and seem more common than they were.

Interestingly, in the 1970s, when polyester became widely available, many museums began using these cheaper, "improved" fabrics for their historical costumes. They soon switched back. Polyester brought several unexpected problems, one of which was its tendency to melt or burn very quickly when it came into contact with flames from candles, hearth fires, or campfires. Traditional fabrics—cotton, linen, and wool—do not easily burst into flame. They tend to smolder, which is probably why there were not more instances of death by petticoat.

Myth #2

Houses didn't have closets in colonial days because people wanted to avoid paying the closet tax.

Ah, that dreaded *closet tax*, striking fear in the hearts of law-abiding colonists! Well . . . not really.

Inventories and floor plans show that many early American houses were built with closets. Typically, they were located on either side of a fireplace in bedrooms and dining rooms, and were used for general storage, not for clothing. Taxes varied widely from colony to colony, and later from state to state, but research has turned up no examples of a tax on closets in any of the thirteen original colonies.

So how were clothes stored? Not on hangers—clothes hangers did not come into use until after the Civil War. Usually, clothing was folded and kept in chests, clothespresses, or chests of drawers, or hung on hooks or nails. People didn't have as much stuff in those days, and even a well-to-do woman would have had just a few dresses.

Today, you can see closets in many historic houses that are open to the public, including Stratford Hall (the Lee home in northern Virginia), Montpelier (the Madison home in Orange, Virginia), and in the Historic Area of Colonial Williamsburg at the Wythe, Randolph, Geddy, and Waller Houses, to name a few. Here, for example, is the floor plan for the Wythe House. See the closets in the two front "chambers," or bedrooms, by the fireplace?

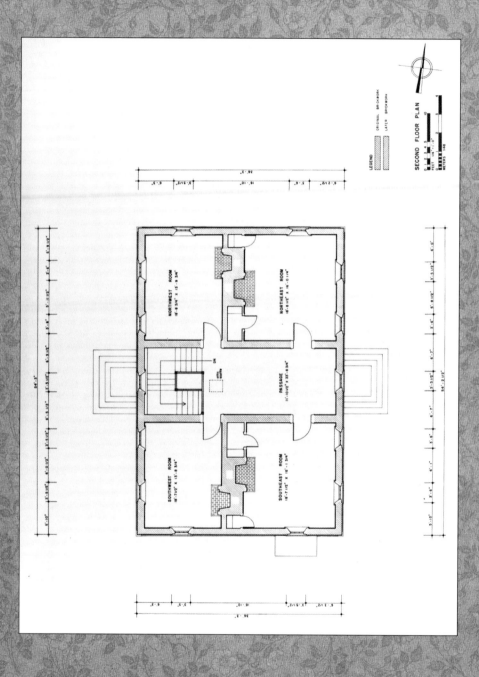

Myth #3

Since most early Americans were illiterate, shop signs had to use pictures instead of words.

This was true in medieval Europe, but not in early America, where pictures on shop and inn signs had more to do with tradition than with mass illiteracy. Most white colonists were literate, though percentages changed over time, and from place to place. The way historians come up with a reasonable estimate is to use a signature as evidence of literacy, a method that isn't perfect, because some people could read but not write, and others could write their names but not read or write much else.

Studies of specific areas give estimates for certain time periods. For instance, in Virginia during the second half of the 1600s, about 60 percent of white men and 25 percent of white women could read. Another study shows that in Williamsburg during the middle of the 1700s, 94 percent of white men and 56 percent of white women could read. In the New England colonies, literacy rates were typically higher than elsewhere because there were more schools, fewer slaves, and a religious tradition that stressed the importance of reading the Bible. Throughout North America, the strongest predictors of literacy were wealth and gender—almost every male head of household who owned property could read and write. In general terms, at the time of the American Revolution, between two-thirds and 90 percent of white men could read, and about half to two-thirds of white women.

Myth #4

Fire screens were placed between a woman and the fireplace to prevent the heat from melting her wax makeup.

elting faces? Yikes! Sounds like a horror movie. Actually, colonial American women wore little or no makeup. European visitors noticed this, and commented on it when they came to America, since wearing makeup was common among upper-class ladies where they came from. If an American woman wanted to wear makeup, she would have had to make it herself. There was no product to purchase in stores. Recipes for skin-care treatment, such as creams intended to be applied and washed off, can be found in household-management books of the period, but none of these used wax as an ingredient.

So what was the point of fire screens? When historians look through inventories (lists of household possessions made after a person's death for legal purposes), they find very few fire screens in early American homes. An expensive accessory, fire screens were often decorated with needlework and placed near the fire for use by men and women to shield them from direct heat. But no one's face was in danger of melting.

Myth #5

**Men posed with one hand inside the vest
to save money, since portrait artists gave a discount
if they didn't have to go to the extra work
of painting the fingers.**

*T*his is a variation of the "arm and a leg" myth: that the expression about something costing an arm and a leg came about because portrait artists charged more if they had to paint the subject's arms or legs. There is no historical verification for either of these myths.

The simple fact is that standing with one hand tucked inside a vest or jacket was a popular, dignified pose for gentlemen and royalty of that era. Do you really think that the Emperor Napoleon, King George, or President George Washington was particularly concerned about getting a discount from a portrait painter?

LE GÉNÉRAL WASHINGTON

Ne Quid Detrimenti capiat Res publica.

Gravé d'après le Tableau Original appartenant a Mr Marquis de la Fayette.

Cette Estampe se Vend avec Privilege du Roy a Paris chez le Mire Graveur rüe et porte St Jacques Maison de M.^r le Camus M.^d de Drap prix 12 livres.

Myth #6

When men smoked tobacco, they often
shared clay pipes. For sanitary reasons,
they would break off the tip of the long stem
before passing the pipe along.

A nd that's why archaeologists find so many bits of broken pipe stems in so many excavations, right?

Well, it certainly makes sense to us today, with our knowledge of germs and the spread of disease. But early Americans didn't know about germs, and so it would not have occurred to them that sharing the same pipe or mug was unsanitary. Yet this myth has survived for decades, probably since someone applied modern logic to explain why archaeologists were unearthing thousands of bits of broken pipe stems at early American sites.

The real reason? The long slender stems of white clay pipes are fragile, as anyone who has handled a reproduction carelessly can attest. Then why did they make them so long? They needed to be long so that the heat from the burning tobacco in the bowls of the pipes would not be conducted as far as the lips. Our forefathers did share pipes, but no one broke off the ends before passing them on.

Myth #7

Early Americans were so religious that they put HL hinges, which stood for Holy Lord, on their doors.

Another version of this story—that the Holy Lord hinges were intended to protect the house from witches—regularly makes the rounds, as well, even in hardware stores!

HL hinges are stronger versions of simple, symmetrical H hinges. The extra supporting arm that fastens to the door helps hold the weight of a heavy wooden door. This arm can be on top, in which case it would look like an HΓ, or on the bottom, where it resembles an L, or it can be mounted on the other side as the mirror image of these two.

Leaving aside the fact that many colonists had little or no interest in religion, no documentation exists for the belief that their hardware had any symbolic value. *H* and *L* referred to the appearance of the hinge. It was not short for Holy Lord.

Myth #8

To ward off witches, early Americans hung doors with Bible and cross symbolism.

According to this myth, the bottom two panels of a six-panel wooden door were designed to represent an open Bible, and the middle stile and rail were meant to form a cross. This story is trotted out to show how pious our ancestors were. Or how laughably superstitious they were to think this would ward off witches.

Remember Myth #7 about the Holy Lord hinges? Same thing here. Both are based on the erroneous belief that all early Americans were very religious and highly superstitious. The truth is, some were and some weren't. But no one at the time thought of his door as Christian symbolism. The six-panel design is just one of many wooden door styles that were popular back then, and it still is today.

Myth #9

Nails were so expensive that people used them on their front doors to show off their wealth.

What is it about doors that attracts so many myths? If it's not the Holy Lord hinges (Myth #7) or the Cross-and-Bible panel door (Myth #8), it's nailing up your front door to show off your wealth.

According to blacksmiths and historians, the truth is the exact *opposite* of this myth. Setting aside the fact that nails were not that expensive (Myth #22), it was the shoddy, cheapest doors that had the most nails. Well-made, more expensive doors show no nails at all.

Myth #10

Beds were shorter back then because people slept sitting up.

This persistent myth has been making the rounds for decades. Truth is, early American beds were made one at a time. There was no standard size. Some beds, especially those for children, were shorter than today's. Some were longer. Some people may have slept propped up on pillows, just as some do today, but beds were not made shorter because of that.

Visitors to a historic house are often surprised if the tour guide takes a measuring tape to a "short" bed and they find it is as long or longer than today's standard seventy-five-inch double bed. Surveys show nearly all antique beds equal or exceed six feet three inches, the standard today. Some are as long as eighty inches, the length of today's king- or queen-size mattresses.

So why do we think the beds are shorter? Because the high bedposts, fabric hangings, canopies, and puffed-up mattresses make them appear that way.

Myth #11

People were shorter back then.

This myth is often heard at historic house museums. For many years, it was false. Now it is true. What happened?

Heights varied in early America as much as they do today, but studies done in the 1960s comparing the average male soldier of the Revolutionary War (1770s) with the average soldier in the Korean War (1950s) found an increase of only about two-thirds of an inch. Interestingly, the average height of colonial American men *does* seem to have been significantly greater than the average height of European men of the same period—up to two inches greater—probably because of better nutrition and healthier living conditions (fewer crowded cities) in the New World.

But recent studies have shown that, in the past half century, the average height of Americans has indeed increased. Comparing soldiers from the Civil War era, who averaged 5 feet 7¼ inches, with today's average for men, 5 feet 10½ inches, shows an increase of more than three inches, most of which occurred in the past fifty years. Vitamins and antibiotics have played a role.

Myth #12

Colonial women were put in pillories for the crime of showing their ankles.

Although there have been many times throughout history when women didn't bare their ankles, the colonial era was not one of them. Skirt length was a matter of both fashion and circumstance. Formal clothing usually involved longer skirts. Work clothing was nearly always shorter for practical reasons. During the workday, a woman might hike up her skirt and tuck the hem into her waist to get it out of the way.

No one went to the pillory for showing her ankles.

Myth #13

The first Thanksgiving was held at Plymouth with the Pilgrims and the Indians in 1621.

That heartwarming tale of Pilgrims and Indians sharing a Thanksgiving feast and prayers at Plymouth never took place. More accurately, it is the combination of two events that did take place: a harvest feast that occurred in 1621 with about ninety Wampanoag Indians and a day of thanksgiving declared by William Bradford in 1623. The pious Pilgrims did not consider the feast a "thanksgiving," which to them meant a solemn day of prayer at church, not a harvest celebration with non-Christians. They would not have combined the two events as we do today.

Besides, was Plymouth really the site of the first Thanksgiving? Not according to Virginians who point to the earlier ceremony at Berkeley Plantation on the James River in 1619. There the settlers followed written instructions to establish the day of their ship's arrival as a day of thanksgiving that would be commemorated every year thereafter. But both these English claims are trumped by the Spanish, who in 1565 in St. Augustine, Florida, celebrated thanksgiving with a Catholic Mass and a meal with the Timucua Indians. Now, now, no squabbling . . . it turns out there were many official days of thanksgiving in colonial America.

By the way, the myth about Indians showing the Pilgrims how to pop corn at Plymouth's first Thanksgiving is another fun story with no basis in fact. Someone made it up more than two hundred years later. And the first *official* Thanksgiving? That didn't happen until Abraham Lincoln made the holiday permanent.

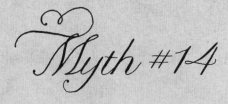

Myth #14

Mirrors were made in two pieces
to avoid the mirror tax.

The fearsome mirror tax, like the closet tax, the second-story tax, and other mythological excise taxes, never existed. The reason large mirrors were made in several pieces was that it was extremely difficult to manufacture large, flat pieces of glass, and even harder to transport them without breaking them. Therefore, it was less expensive to make mirrors in two pieces.

The legend may have its origin in the Townshend Revenue Acts of 1767, which set taxes on certain imported items coming from England to the American colonies, including plate glass. Plate glass was used for both mirrors and large windows. But Parliament repealed the Townshend Duties after the colonists protested (except for the tax on tea, and we all know how that turned out), so any duties on glass were never collected. There was no excise tax in the thirteen colonies on mirrors.

Myth #15

Early Americans thought tomatoes were poisonous.

*I*t's hard to imagine the Italians without tomato sauce, isn't it? But no one in Europe knew about tomatoes until Spanish explorers discovered the "tomatl" growing in Central America. They thought it was delicious, and brought it back from their voyages. During the 1500s, the tomato spread from Spain and Portugal to Italy and France, where it became quite popular. But in 1597, a rather unreliable British barber–surgeon published a book about plants in which he claimed the tomato was poisonous, even though he also noted that the French and Italians ate the thing. Presumably these particular Europeans weren't quite human. This book set the stage for the negative view of tomatoes among the English that lasted more than a century. However, by the end of the 1700s, tomatoes had overcome this bad press.

Another myth claims that Thomas Jefferson brought the tomato to America, or that his friend Dr. John deSequeyra did. Jefferson did grow tomatoes, and Dr. deSequeyra was probably first to bring tomatoes to the Virginia colony, but no single person was responsible for introducing them to North America. Immigrants from countries where the tomato flourished—France, Spain, Portugal, and the Caribbean islands—brought them wherever they settled. Jewish merchants played a significant role because they were widely engaged in international trade, and because most were of Spanish or Portuguese descent and had long been familiar with tomatoes.

So, yes, in the 1600s, some Englishmen in England and America probably thought the tomato was poisonous. By the 1700s, they had wised up. The Italians, French, Portuguese, and Spanish never deluded themselves into thinking there was any danger in tomatoes.

Myth #16

Potatoes were considered poisonous by early colonists.

*Y*ou say tomato, I say to-mah-to! You say potato, I say po-tah-to! The poisonous-potato myth runs along the same lines as the poisonous-tomato myth—somewhat true in the 1500s, but by the time the English were colonizing the North American coast, the fear had gone.

The potato came to Europe from South America in 1562 with a long list of supposed side effects. Some thought it caused leprosy or was associated with the devil. Others claimed it protected against rheumatism or worked as an aphrodisiac. A few thought it was poisonous. According to legend, Sir Walter Raleigh got sick eating the poisonous potato berries, not realizing that the edible part grows underground. He demanded the plant be destroyed. The servant who burned it accidentally cooked the underground potato, tasted it, and found it delicious. But the tale is impossible, since Raleigh never visited a potato-producing region in his life.

One part rings true—the potato does contain a natural toxin in its leaves, stem, and green spots on the skin. It is certainly possible that someone ate the wrong part and got sick. Others spurned the vegetable because it wasn't mentioned in the Bible, or because it resembled a leper's deformed fingers and toes.

By the 1700s, potatoes were an important part of the European diet, in part because they could be left underground until needed, like a food bank account, protected from thieves, foraging armies, or greedy tax collectors who either couldn't see them or didn't want to take the time to dig them up.

Myth #17

The Dutch bought Manhattan from the Indians for $24 worth of worthless beads.

*N*ope.

Only one original piece of evidence tells us anything about the purchase of Manhattan: a letter written in 1626 by merchant Pieter Schagen to the West India Company (the owners of New Netherland, now New York) saying that the settlers "have bought the island of Manhattes from the savages for a value of 60 guilders." That's all we know for certain. It doesn't say which settlers purchased the island, or from whom they purchased it, although it was probably the local Lenape tribe. Typically, the trade goods Indians most desired were things like axes, iron kettles, copper, and wool fabric. No reason beads couldn't have been included, but nothing tells us exactly what the mix was. North American Indians were notoriously shrewd traders and would not have been fooled by worthless trinkets.

A little more is known about the purchase of Staten Island. That sale was also made for sixty guilders' worth of goods, and this time we know the Indians got cloth, axes, hoes, awls, kettles, Jew's harps, and beads. The Manhattan mix was probably similar.

North American Indians and Europeans had very different ideas about land ownership. The Indians regarded land as something you could use but not own or sell, like air or water. Some historians have suggested that the Indians may have thought they were sharing, not selling.

Myth #18

The Good Friday Massacre of 1622 took place on Good Friday.

On the morning of March 22, 1622, Virginia's Powhatan Indian alliance executed a well-coordinated attack on English settlements spread fifty miles up and down the James River. Warriors from a dozen tribes fell on men, women, and children in their homes and fields, burning houses and barns, killing livestock, and mutilating the bodies of their victims. Planned by the Pamunkey headman Opechancanough, the offensive slew about 350 people, one-sixth of the total in the fifteen-year-old colony, but failed in its purpose. It did not stop the English invaders who were taking Indian land and massacring Indians.

The raid is commonly called the Good Friday Massacre—a catchy name, to be sure, but the trouble is, it didn't happen on Good Friday. Or anywhere near that date. That year, Easter fell on April 21, making April 19 Good Friday—four weeks *after* the uprising.

So how did this myth begin? Back in 1871, a careless clergyman wrote a book, mixing up the date of Opechancanough's *second* surprise attack (the one in 1644 that actually did occur near Easter, though on the Thursday before Easter, not on Good Friday) with the first. The clergyman accidentally moved the attack of 1644 by one day—to Good Friday—and confused that with the date of the first attack in 1622. Sadly, his mistake lives on in school textbooks and Internet sites, despite the efforts of historians to set the record straight.

Myth #19

Most men wore wigs in colonial America.

*N*ot by a long shot. Most men did *not* wear wigs. Even if they had wanted to, a wig was a very expensive fashion accessory. And not all those who could afford to wear a wig did so. Many preferred to arrange and powder their own hair.

Experts estimate that only about 5 percent of the American population wore wigs, about half of them well-to-do landowners and half from the "middling sort," or tradesmen and professionals such as lawyers, doctors, merchants, ship captains, and teachers. Some ladies of the upper class wore wigs, too, but not many. Believe it or not, a few advertisements for runaway slaves mentioned the slaves were wearing wigs.

And what about that expression "Don't flip your wig"? Some claim it originated in the eighteenth century as a warning against groveling—bowing so low to a superior that your wig flipped off. Instead, the phrase seems to be a bit of twentieth-century American slang meaning "to go crazy," and the earliest known use of the phrase occurred in the 1950s. On the other hand, the word "blockhead" is a colonial-era insult. Wooden forms used as wig stands, like the one pictured here and in Myth #20, were known as blockheads.

Myth #20

Wigs were baked in loaves of bread to set the hair.

This sounds so absurd, it must be a myth, right? Well, it is, technically speaking. But there is a kernel of truth here that shows just how this myth got started.

Turning real hair into a wig required many steps: taking fresh hanks of hair, rolling them onto white clay curlers, tying them with string, and boiling them in water. How to dry them? In an oven, since hair dryers did not exist. For customers who wanted the frizzy-style wig that was so popular with clergymen and lawyers, there was an extra step.

In his 1767 book, *Art of the Wigmaker,* Monsieur de Garsault described the process. After boiling and drying the hair curlers, he arranged them in layers in "the form of a loaf" and wrapped them in cheesecloth. Tying the package with string, he took it to a baker, who "surrounds it with a paste of rye flour, puts it in a moderate oven and bakes it. The 'loaf' being cooked, and sent back to you whilst hot, break it open and remove all the 'sets.'" By calling the bunch of curlers a "loaf" and by mentioning a paste of rye flour and an oven, it seems Garsault accidentally started the rumor that wigs were baked inside loaves of bread.

To summarize: Although whole wigs were not baked inside loaves of bread, bunches of curls were heated in ovens to dry and frizz them. To protect the hair, these curls were encased in a flour paste.

Myth #21

Fear of fire caused early Americans to build the kitchen separate from the main house.

Kitchens burned down all the time, and a kitchen is easier to replace than your whole house, right? But records show that kitchens didn't really burn down all that often, and if fear of fire was the main reason for putting the kitchen in a separate building from the main house, how come only the people living in the South feared fire? Separate kitchens were not a common feature in northern colonies, but they were very common in the South. And by the way, the main house had several fireplaces, so where's the logic?

Actual reasons had more to do with the heat and odors from the kitchen fire, which would not have been welcome in the hot, humid South. Hugh Jones, a mathematics teacher at the College of William and Mary, noted in 1724 that planters often kept their "kitchen apart from the dwelling house, because of the smell of hot victuals, offensive in hot weather." Another reason was the desire to segregate kitchen slaves from the family's main living space. Cooks and other slaves worked in the kitchen all day, and usually slept in the loft or second story.

Myth #22

Handwrought iron nails were so valuable in the American colonies that people burned down buildings just to collect the nails.

*H*ere's a good example of how a myth gets started. There is often a nugget of truth if you dig deep enough . . . back to a single law in the 1640s that prohibited the burning of buildings for the nails.

During the earliest years of the Virginia colony, buildings were constructed in a very slipshod manner, with wood sitting directly on the ground. They were meant to be temporary, because the young male settlers hadn't planned to settle at all—they had come to make a quick fortune and go home. So they built shacks that quickly rotted. Occasionally the settlers got rid of these shacks by burning them, and afterward, nothing stopped them from sifting through the ashes for the nails. The nails weren't all that valuable, but why waste them?

The law aimed to protect against fires spreading out of control, so authorities offered to give a man the number of nails estimated to be in a shack if he would refrain from burning it. Did this work? We don't really know. However, slipshod building techniques soon gave way to sounder ones. No one ever burned a decent building for a handful of inexpensive nails.

Myth #23

The first settlers built log cabins.

They couldn't build log cabins. They didn't know how.
The first Europeans who settled America's eastern
seaboard were the Spanish in Florida (1565), the French in
Canada (1605), and the English in Virginia (1607). None of these
newcomers came from a culture that used logs to build homes, so
they built the sort of houses they were familiar with: wooden frame
houses, or brick, or wattle and daub (wooden strips filled in with a
mud-and-straw mixture).

Log cabins came later, when Scandinavians began immigrating
to New Sweden, the colony located in present-day Delaware
and New Jersey, in 1638. These folks constructed traditional,
Scandinavian-style log houses. Simple and quick to build, the style
caught on with other ethnic groups, becoming the default house
for pioneers on the woodland frontier.

Myth #24

Apprenticeships lasted seven years.

*W*ell ... sometimes.

Looking through surviving apprentice contracts like the one pictured here shows that there was no set time span for an apprenticeship in colonial America. Some contracts specify a certain number of years, such as four, six, or seven. Others say the apprentice will work until he has reached twenty-one, no matter his age at the start. In the example here, a boy named Thomas Callahan was apprenticed for eight years and ten months (see line 7). Evidence suggests that family apprenticeships—a man training a son or a younger brother—tended to be shorter than average. Occasionally, girls were apprenticed to learn millinery or housewifery skills.

After completing the apprenticeship, the young person could work for wages as a journeyman or, if he had the means, set up on his own as a master—a tradesman who had his own shop. A master was not necessarily more skilled than a journeyman; the word meant that he worked for himself rather than for someone else. Some tradesmen, such as barbers and bookbinders, needed a relatively small investment in tools and overhead to set up shop. Others, such as cabinetmakers, printers, and goldsmiths, required a good deal of start-up capital, making it difficult for a journeyman to become a master.

This Indenture Witnesseth..

That Thomas Callahan Of the County Of Campbell & State Of Virgena, Hath Put himself And By these present. Doth put Himself. Agreable. To an Order. Of Court. An Apprentice Unto William weber Citizen and Blacksmith Of Said County & State Afforesaid. To Learn his Art Trade Or Mistry. And After the the Manner Of An Apprentice To Serve him from the Day of the Date Hereof for and During the Term Of Eighty years and Ten Months Next Ensuing; During all which Time He the Said Apprentice his Master Shall faithfully Serve, his Secrets keep his Lawfull Commands Obey, he shall do No Damage To his Sd Master Nor See it To be Done by Others, Without Letting Or Giving Notice To his Sd Master. He shall Wast his Said Masters Goods Nor Lend them Unlawfully To Others. he Shall Not Commit fornication Nor Contract Matrimoney Within the Sd Term. At Cards Dice Or Any Unlawfull Game he Shall Not play, Whereby his Sd Master May Be Damaged With his Own Goods Or the Goods Of Others During the The Sd Term, Without License Of his Sd Master. He Shall Neither Buy Nor Sell, he shall not Absent himself Day Nor Night from his Sd Masters Service without his Leave, Nor haunt Ale houses, Taverns or Play houses, But In All things behave himself As A faithfull Apprentice Ought to Do during the Sd term. And the Sd Master Shall Use the Utmost Of his Endeavours, To teach Or Cause To be taught And Instructed the Sd Apprentice In the Trade and Mistry Of A Blacksmith And procure and provide for him the Sd Apprentice Sufficient Meat Drink Washing Lodging and Apparrel Together With Giving him Learning Such Or Redding Writeing and Arithmetick As far As the Rule Of Three Together With Freedom Dues. To the Amount Of Three Pound Ten Shilling And for the True performance Of All And Every the Sd Covenants And Agreements Either Of the Sd parties Bind themselves Unto The Other by these presents.

In Witness Whereof We have Interchangeably Set Our Hands and Seals this Xth Day Of June In the Year Of Our Lord, 793, And In the Seventeenth Year Of Our Independance

Witness

Christopher Irvine

Myth #25

Early Americans used the blue paper that wrapped their sugarloaves to dye fabric.

A sweet story, but experts in historic crafts and housewifery skills say that no examples of dyeing yarn or fabric with purplish-blue wrapping paper are known in early America. It's downright illogical. White sugar was an expensive, imported luxury—think caviar—that only the wealthy could afford . . . not the sort of people who would be recycling packaging to dye their own clothes.

However, several books published in the nineteenth century do mention this practice. In one of them, *The American Frugal Housewife* from 1835, author Lydia Childs describes how to make various cheap dyes, including "a fine purple slate color" by boiling sugar wrapping paper in vinegar with alum. Why then and not earlier? Probably because that's when sugar became cheap. The expansion of Caribbean sugar plantations flooded the market and prices dropped, bringing sugarloaves, wrapped in traditional purplish-blue paper, within reach of most housewives. So this myth is false when heard at early American sites and true for later, nineteenth-century sites.

Before white sugar was affordable, what did Americans use for sweeteners? Maple sugar, honey, molasses, or unrefined muscovado sugar. Or more likely, nothing.

Myth #26

Venetian blinds were invented in Venice.

Sounds like a slam dunk, doesn't it? But only English people called these adjustable window blinds *Venetian*. Italians called them *persiana*. The French called them *jalousie a la persienne*. This suggests that they originated in the Middle East, in the Persian Empire, or perhaps beyond, in China or India. They probably got the English name "Venetian blinds" from coming to Europe via Venice, the port city that handled most of the trade with the East.

Whenever anyone thinks of Venice's trade with the East, they think of Marco Polo, an association that probably gave rise to the legend that he brought them back to Venice from China. Again, there is no evidence. Polo's own writings tell of the many wonders he experienced during his Asian travels, but he doesn't mention window blinds. And frankly, it seems like a long, long delay between the time he spent in China in the late 1200s and when the blinds appeared in Europe almost five hundred years later.

Here's a story that *is* true: Thrifty George Washington wanted the fashionable new Venetian blinds for his Mount Vernon home. He ordered *one* to fit a dining room window, intending to learn from that one so that "others may be made by it at home."

Myth #27

Colonial Americans suffered from widespread lead poisoning due to the lead in their pewter.

*T*his is a myth. Sort of.

You probably know that pewter is made mostly of tin. You may also know that it *can* contain lead, but not always. The secondary metal can be copper, antimony, brass, zinc, bismuth, or lead. Good-quality eighteenth-century pewter contained no lead, but the lower-quality stuff sometimes did.

Everyone was exposed to pewter in the form of plates, utensils, and drinking vessels. Even well-to-do folks who could afford sterling silver and ceramics on their dining tables were exposed, because pewter was used in their kitchens. Colonists also came into daily contact with lead through lead-glazed pottery, lead crystal, musket balls, lead paint, and lead solder. With so many sources of lead, it is hard to pin the blame on one in particular. It seems safe to say that some pewter *contributed* to lead poisoning but was not the most significant source.

Did the colonists realize the lead in their pewter played a role in their health problems? Almost certainly not. Was lead poisoning widespread? Studies measuring lead levels in old bones show some were high, but others were not.

Pewter gradually faded from everyday use, replaced by ceramic plates and glass drinking vessels made cheaply through the efficiencies of mass production. Don't worry about using any modern pewter you may own—it's lead free. Antiques and foreign imports are a little riskier, since there is no easy way to tell whether those include lead. Save them for display.

Myth #28

During the Revolutionary War, people melted pewter mugs and plates to make bullets.

ince we're already on the subject of deadly pewter ... what about pewter bullets?

Bullet molds were intended to make lead bullets, but historians and firearms experts say that, in a pinch, you *could* use pewter even though it would be inferior to lead. However, no one has been able to point to an actual, historical example. Yes, a few old books and family genealogies claim this occurred during the Revolutionary War, but it's easy to repeat stories and family lore, harder to find proof in the form of a primary source.

Besides, pewter wouldn't work well at all. With bullets, heavier is better. Pewter would work—heck, aluminum foil would work—but pewter is mostly tin with a small amount of another metal, sometimes lead, but not always. Imagine the power of a tin bullet. It wouldn't go as far as a lead one, it would lose speed more quickly, and it wouldn't have much energy when it struck. In dire emergencies, melting down one's pewter plates might have provided ammunition that was better than throwing snowballs, but a well-aimed rock would probably do more damage.

Even though this *might* have occurred on rare occasion, the statement makes it sound commonplace and deserves to be judged a myth.

Now Dress and Ornament the Female's Pride?
No longer can their powerfull Influence hide.

NOON.

The Toilet now and Glass exert their Arts;
What less the Conquest than a thousand Hearts

London Printed for Rob.t Sayer, opposite Fetter Lane Fleet Street.

Myth #29

Women ate arsenic to lighten their complexions.

No, but they did something just as bad. For nearly three hundred years, some upper-class European women used a lead-based makeup to lighten their skin.

Unlike the late twentieth century when everyone wanted a "healthy" tan, in earlier centuries people thought pale was prettier. Pale skin was a status symbol. It showed that the person didn't have to work outside in the fields like a peasant. But there is no evidence that supports the rumor that women ate arsenic to lighten their skin. In fact, arsenic actually darkens the skin, so anyone trying this would have abandoned the effort quickly. Or died.

Starting in the early 1500s, some wealthy European women (think Queen Elizabeth I) used a skin lightener called ceruse. Made with white lead, ceruse was also used in making paint. This caused damage, perhaps death, if the woman applied it often enough. It was still available in France in the middle 1700s. American women of that period also valued pale skin, but they did not typically wear makeup of any kind. There is no evidence that American women applied ceruse to their faces.

Myth #30

Many houses and roads in America were built with bricks and stones carried here as ballast in the holds of ships.

*E*xaggerated, but fundamentally true.

A ship needs ballast when it isn't carrying enough weight to keep upright. In early America, there was sometimes more cargo going to England, especially from the tobacco- and cotton-producing South, than there was coming into those colonies. So incoming ships sometimes had to carry ballast.

Because of sensible laws against dumping ballast in a river or at a port (think how quickly that would clog the waterways!), ship captains knew to take ballast they could unload and sell on arrival. Records show that bricks were sometimes used, as was slate, coal, and flagstones, even though such things were usually available in America. The most common ballast was stone, which was sometimes just piled along the waterfront after it had served its purpose.

But quantities were relatively small. For instance, records mention "ten thousand bricks" or "100 feet of flagstone." A large house might require 250,000 bricks and a chimney, 6,000 to 8,000, making it unlikely that any building was constructed entirely from ballast. Some riverfront warehouses in Savannah, Georgia, have ballast stone foundations, and a house in Maryland has ballast stones in part of one wall. As for paving roads, South Carolina historians have proof that ballast was available for street paving in Charleston after 1784. And during the 1800s, ballast paved some of the sandy waterfront streets in Savannah, Georgia. When supplies of ballast ran out in the 1880s, Savannah had to buy its paving stones.

So when the guide driving your horse-drawn carriage tells you that all the cobblestone streets were paved with ballast, you'll smile and nod and know he's exaggerating.

Myth #31

Cooks used spices to mask the flavor and odors of rotting food.

Sometimes this statement is made about the medieval era and sometimes about colonial days. Either way, it is false.

Spices we consider common today were once hugely expensive, imported from the so-called Spice Islands (Indonesia, Sri Lanka, Malaysia, and others) on the other side of the world. For centuries, only the rich could afford such luxuries as pepper, nutmeg, cinnamon, and cloves . . . not the sort of people who ate spoiled meat.

Spices were so valuable they were kept in small boxes or cupboards, often under lock and key. People used them sparingly, not as a cover-up.

Myth #32

A man's suit of clothes cost a year's wages.

To show how expensive clothing was in colonial America, it is occasionally said that a journeyman (a tradesman who worked for wages) had to spend an entire year's wages just to buy a single suit of clothes. Well, maybe if he had an audience with the king . . .

Like today, clothing was available at a wide range of prices. Everything was handmade, and new clothing could be costly, but used clothing could be had for next to nothing. People in general owned far less clothing than we do today. Even the well-to-do had just a few outfits. Upper-class women might remake their dresses by sending them out to be dyed different colors and then attaching new trimmings. Regular folks may have had only one or two changes of clothing. The poor often had only what was on their backs. A colonial tailor from Alexandria, Virginia, who made clothes for field hands as well as the planter elite charged £3 to £5 for an ordinary wool suit, and £15 for a silk brocade suit. Meanwhile, a journeyman's annual wages around the time of the Revolution averaged £30 to £35.

Myth #33

Wearing blue- or green-tinted eyeglasses meant the wearer had syphilis.

*H*onestly, now, if someone had syphilis, would he or she want to advertise it to the world?

Tinted eyeglasses are not a recent invention. In the 1700s, some people wore blue, green, amber, or amethyst lenses to protect their eyes from the sun's glare. This did not indicate a medical problem.

Medical books of the time mention various treatments for syphilis, but none suggest using colored lenses. The disease can cause eye damage, so perhaps that's where the myth began.

Myth #34

Panes of window glass in old buildings are visibly thicker at the bottom, proving that glass is a viscous liquid that "flows" or sags over time.

The National Park Service, various physicists, and even Wikipedia have been trying to squelch this myth for years. Antique glass was made by hand. Craftsmen tried to make each plate of glass evenly flat, but there was often visible variation in the thickness. One early technique, pictured here, involved spinning molten glass to create a round, flat plate. The edges could turn out thicker than the middle. The cooled plate was then cut to fit a windowpane. If one edge was thicker, the installer generally placed that edge down for stability. If you look closely at a piece of antique window glass, you may see a faint arc, not to mention bubbles or other imperfections, all of which are evidence of hand craftsmanship.

If glass really did flow visibly over time, we would see more flow in ancient Egyptian glass than we do in, say, colonial American glass. But that is not the case. A few years ago, a physicist tried to calculate the time required for glass to actually flow, and found that at 777°F, the glass would move a visible amount in eight hundred years. At room temperature, it would take longer than the age of the universe.

Pl. XVI.

Fig. 1.

a

b

Fig. 2.

a

b

e

c

Radel Del.

Benard Fecit.

Q

Verrerie en bois,
l'Opération de plotter le plat et de le faire recuire au Four.

Myth #35

Corner chairs were designed to accommodate men wearing swords.

orner chairs were often used in a corner or at a desk. They were not terribly rare—you can find antique examples at many museums and in period houses, where they are usually found in bedchambers, sitting rooms, or libraries. They were also called roundabout chairs, smoking chairs, barber's chairs, writing chairs, and desk chairs—names that suggest men were the primary users. But not men wearing swords.

Like so many fashions, corner chairs became popular first in England in the early years of the eighteenth century and then spread to the American colonies. Most of these chairs were made from about 1730 to the 1790s, after which their popularity declined.

However, men almost never wore swords indoors, so the corner chair was not invented to deal with this "problem." Re-enactors and living-history participants who have tried sitting in a corner chair while wearing a sword claim that it is actually harder to use these chairs than regular ones.

If you come across a corner chair with a particularly deep seat rail, it was probably used as a commode chair (also known as a night chair, a necessary chair, or a closestool), with a chamber pot fixed below the removable seat. The deep seat rail hid the chamber pot.

MARYE the QUEENE.

Myth #36

Chairs without arms were designed to accommodate women wearing wide hoop skirts.

Another chair myth! Armchairs were an indication of status and were reserved for the head of the household or other important people. Think of a king's throne, with its high back and arms. Armchairs were rare. Most people of average or low status sat on backless benches or stools.

Chairs without arms (usually called side chairs today) first appeared in the 1500s. Sometime during the 1800s, people started calling them "farthingale chairs," mistakenly linking the chair's purpose to the wide hoops ladies once wore. Wide hoops did not make it hard for women to sit in armchairs—just look at the portraits that show Queen Elizabeth I or her half-sister, Queen Mary I (shown here), wearing bulky gowns and seated in thrones, which are nothing more than fancy armchairs.

Myth #37

Cabinetmakers built furniture with doors that had thirteen panes of glass to represent the original thirteen states of the United States.

Some objects, such as the American flag and the dollar bill, *were* designed to represent the thirteen original states. Glass-paned cupboard doors are not further examples.

Occasionally, furniture made in England in the Chinese style did have glass-paned doors with thirteen panes, but the English certainly weren't doing so to celebrate their loss of the thirteen American colonies. A furniture-design book by Thomas Chippendale, published in England twenty-three years before the American Revolution, shows large pieces with doors that have thirteen panes of glass. Others have six panes, or twenty-seven, or just about any number. Thirteen is just coincidence.

Myth #38

Ice cream was invented in (fill in the location) by (fill in the name).

There are more myths about ice cream than flavors at an ice cream parlor. Some say the ancient Romans invented it, others that Marco Polo brought it to Italy from China, or that Catherine de Medici introduced it to the French when she married the future king Henry II. Not to be outdone by Europeans, Americans have claimed ice cream was first made by Martha Washington, Thomas Jefferson, or Dolley Madison. All of these stories were created during the nineteenth century by ice cream sellers looking for a marketing angle.

Sure, each contains a kernel of truth. The Romans *did* mix chipped ice with various flavorings, but that makes snow cones, not ice cream. Marco Polo *did* visit China in the thirteenth century, but he makes no mention of ice cream in his journals. And Catherine de Medici *did* become queen of France, but that was more than a century before the first French ice cream recipe showed up.

Ice cream probably originated in China. Its European debut probably took place in Italy in the late 1600s, then spread through the royal houses of Europe. The first *known* instance of ice cream in America occurred in 1744, when Maryland's governor served it for dessert. Jefferson encountered ice cream in Paris. Delighted, he brought home a recipe, and on Independence Day 1806 served it at the White House. For many people, this was their introduction to ice cream, hence the belief that Jefferson brought the dish to America. Martha Washington did not invent ice cream any more than Jefferson or Dolley Madison, but she served it at Mount Vernon on many occasions.

Myth #39

A silver item stamped COIN means it was made from melting down silver coins.

Occasionally, yes, coins were used as a source for silver: A rare example would be the time that George Washington had a dozen small silver camp cups made from sixteen silver dollars. But the word "coin" stamped onto silver objects means the silver was the same proportion as that used for coinage, or 900 parts per thousand, as opposed to the higher 925 parts per thousand for sterling silver. The remaining portion of the alloy was usually copper, needed to strengthen pure silver, which otherwise would have been too soft.

When the American colonies belonged to England, they of course followed English laws in marking their silver. After independence, standards varied among the different states. In 1837, Congress passed a law that established 900/1000 as the official ratio for coin silver.

See Elmer's spoon? And see the word "coin" stamped to the left of Elmer's name? This let people know that the silver content in the spoon was the same as in the coinage, or 900 parts per thousand. Elmer's spoon—like most other items similarly marked—was almost certainly *not* made from melted coins.

Myth #40

In olden days, shoes were made straight,
not as rights and lefts, so they could be rotated
as we rotate tires and would wear evenly.

*I*t depends on which olden days you're referring to.
Back in Shakespeare's day, the wooden forms that shoes
were made on changed from left and right to straight. Why? To
economize, so that shoemakers would need only one form to make
a pair of shoes. This situation lasted until around 1800, when forms
started to go right and left again. So, for about two hundred years,
most English and American shoes were made on straight forms.

But even straight-made shoes will quickly conform to the
wearer's feet and turn a little right or left, so shoes were *not* rotated
for the purpose of wearing evenly.

Myth #41

The most stylish shoes were made of dog skin, hence the expression "puttin' on the dog."

Sticking with the shoe topic for a moment, let's bust this one about dog leather. Cruella de Vil aside, no one used dog skin to make shoes or boots in America. (That isn't to say that it never happens—recent newspaper stories have told about dogs slaughtered for their skins in South Asia today, but here we're dealing with American history myths.)

So what is the origin of the phrase "puttin' on the dog"? Evidently, the expression got started in the middle of the nineteenth century, and it means "to show off." Similar phrases were "putting on the ritz" or "cut a swell." The earliest known use of the phrase was at Yale University in 1871, where it is said to have been college slang meaning "make a flashy display." Or to show off. Nothing to do with dog-skin shoes.

Myth #42

Itinerant portrait painters would paint incomplete pictures of headless bodies so they could save time when they found clients, adding only the heads.

Such a good idea! Stay home during the winter months and paint a stock of canvases with bodies and backgrounds, then ride out in the warmer months to find clients who could select bodies and pay to have their heads painted on them. A real time-saver for both artist and sitters, right?

But there is no evidence for it. No artist or sitter mentioned this practice in diaries or other written records. No unfinished, headless portrait painted by an early American folk artist has been discovered in an attic or storage shed. (The few unfinished portraits that do survive include heads.) And no physical evidence, such as overlapping paint layers at the neck or head, has been detected on existing portraits. Nonetheless, museum guides say that someone in each group inevitably asks about this whenever folk-art portraits come into view.

It makes sense to us today; and it seems to explain the similarities in the clothing and backgrounds of some American folk-art portraits. However, in portrait painting, artists typically start with the most important feature—the head—and work the rest around that.

Myth #43

Women secluded themselves indoors during pregnancy.

This persistent falsehood is trotted out for American women in both the colonial and the Victorian eras. There is little evidence to support the claim in either period, although some women did seclude themselves after a child was born.

Poor and middle-class women simply couldn't afford to remain indoors for months on end—for crying out loud, they had too much work to do! Wealthy women, who theoretically *could* have stayed indoors, did not want to. Not only did pregnant women venture outside their homes, but they also enjoyed active social lives, dining with friends, attending religious services and cultural events, and going about their daily business. Letters and diaries of the period provide ample evidence.

So where did this myth come from? Popular fiction, such as *Gone with the Wind,* may have contributed to the idea. Author Margaret Mitchell wrote that Scarlett O'Hara was criticized for appearing in public while pregnant: "No respectable white woman and few negroes ever went outside their homes from the moment they first suspected they were with child." But that's fiction. Actual historical records paint a very different picture.

Myth #44

Before the days of hospitals, houses had designated birthing rooms.

*U*ntil the twentieth century, women gave birth at home, usually in their own beds in their own bedrooms. There were no special birthing rooms reserved for this purpose, even in the largest, most elegant houses.

Pregnancy was a time of great stress for women because of the many problems that could occur with both baby and mother. An estimated one in eight colonial women died in childbirth. About half of their babies died before their fifth birthdays.

An interesting note: Many women returned to their parents' homes to give birth, especially for a first child. This wasn't some sentimental tradition—it made it possible for experienced mothers and sisters to assist with deliveries.

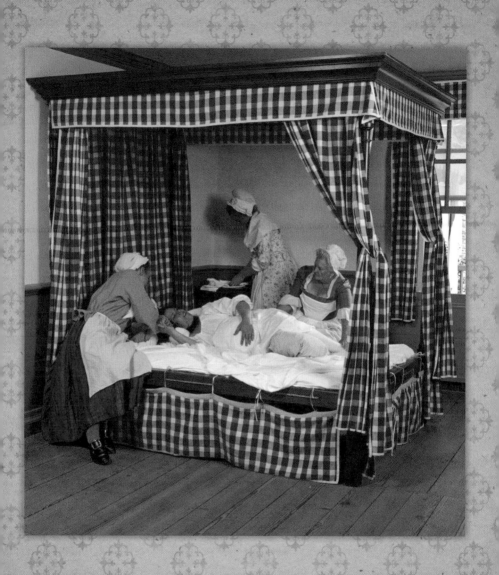

Myth #45

The position of a horse's legs on an equestrian statue tells how the rider died.

Pssst. There's a secret statue code that tells the rider's fate by the position of his horse's legs. If one hoof is raised, the soldier was wounded in battle. It two hooves are raised, he died in battle. If all four hooves are on the ground, he survived the battle or war.

What makes this myth so amusing is that anyone can look around at the statues and see that reality bears little relationship to the "secret code." In Washington, DC, the American city with the most statues, one-third follow the code. Seeing as how there are three possibilities, it seems chance is hard at work. In Gettysburg, a battlefield full of statues, most of the horses actually do conform to the code, but not all. For example, General James Longstreet wasn't wounded in that battle but his horse has one leg raised.

The myth may have started at Gettysburg. If you looked at three or four statues and found the pattern held true, you might conclude all the rest did, too. And we are all suckers for any sort of secret code, so it naturally sticks in our minds.

The equestrian-statues code seems to be an American version of an older, English code that uses the position of the legs of the knights on their tombs to indicate whether they went on Crusade. Historians have pointed to many examples where this is clearly wrong, but the myth won't die.

Myth #46

It was against the law to teach African-Americans, enslaved or free, to read.

Sometimes true, sometimes not, depending upon where and when.

During the colonial period in Virginia, no laws prohibited teaching slaves to read. In fact, Samuel Davies, a Presbyterian minister, worked hard to bring books and education to Virginia slaves in the mid-1700s. A teacher named Mrs. Wager taught black children—most enslaved, some free—at the Bray School in Williamsburg from 1760 until her death in 1774. Unlike the all-white, all-male College of William and Mary down the street, Mrs. Wager taught boys *and* girls.

In colonial South Carolina, teaching a slave to write was not illegal until 1740, the year after the Stono Slave Rebellion. Georgia passed a similar law in 1755. Slaves who knew how to read and write could more easily communicate plans for uprisings. But in most colonies, north and south, a slave's education was left up to the owner.

In the 1800s, most southern states passed laws against teaching African-Americans, slave or free. For example, in 1831, Virginia passed a harsh law that limited the activities of the enslaved population and put education out of reach for most. In 1833, Alabama tried to cover all bases with a law fining anyone who taught a slave or free person of color to spell, read, or write. Before the Civil War, about 10 percent of African-Americans could read; immediately after, the percentage jumped to 30 percent as former slaves rushed to learn.

So, generally speaking, teaching African-Americans was
usually legal in southern colonies and states until about 1830. After
that, it was usually illegal.

Myth #47

Double staircases were designed so that men could use one side and women the other, to avoid accidental glimpses of ankles.

*A*h, those naked ankles! Seems anywhere you have a double staircase this myth pops up. The idea is that Victorian men and women were so prudish they couldn't risk a glimpse of ankle. Trouble is, many of the houses with double staircases were built long before the Victorian age.

Most large historic houses have two staircases. The nicer one was meant for the family and guests; the smaller, narrower, steeper one was for servants and slaves. You didn't want to run into servants carrying chamber pots, dirty laundry, or hot water up and down the stairs.

Another sort of double staircase is the mirror-image kind built—often outside—on very grand mansions and palaces, such as Fontainebleau in France. Pictured is an example from Berry Hill, an 1835 home in Halifax County, Virginia. Decorative double staircases like these were designed to impress, not for modesty.

Myth #48

Western pioneers kept their clothing in chests rather than wardrobes because wardrobes were taxed as extra rooms.

*Y*ou'll hear this blooper out west, particularly in Utah, where Park Service rangers are trying to stamp out the claim that the Mormon pioneers lived in one-room cabins without wardrobes because wardrobes were taxed as second rooms. Shunning taxes and wardrobes, thrifty pioneers put their clothing in chests or trunks instead, right?

Alert readers will recognize this as a variant of the closet tax (Myth #2) or the second-story tax, but is there even a remote sliver of truth to it?

Utah's early territorial laws from 1847 to 1888 do not mention wardrobes or extra rooms at all. In fact, the Compiled Laws of Utah, 1888, specifically *exempts* each family from being taxed on any "wearing apparel, beds, bedding, stoves, chairs, etc. not exceeding one hundred dollars," and that would include furniture such as wardrobes. It is unlikely that pioneers living in a one-room house would have owned more than $100 worth of "stuff," so they would have paid no personal-property taxes. A few years later, household furniture was no longer taxable at all.

So, yes, for a very short time, household furniture worth more than $100 total was taxed in some parts of the Utah Territory. But not wardrobes per se, and certainly not because they were considered a second room. This myth isn't limited to Utah—any western state is fair game.

Early American guns were very heavy and awkward to fire.

uite the opposite. A standard British military gun of the eighteenth century weighed about the same as the U.S. Army's nine-and-a-half-pound World War II rifle, the M1 Garand. Gunsmiths say that the weight of most early American guns ranged from six to ten pounds. They were not particularly heavy. Nor did folks at the time consider them awkward to fire, although today we would find the loading process cumbersome.

Myth #50

Stairs were sometimes built with one riser noticeably shorter than the rest to trip up burglars.

*I*t would make a great movie scene, wouldn't it? In the dead of night, a thief breaks quietly into the house. Sneaking up the stairs, he comes down hard on one foot when one of the stair risers is unexpectedly shorter than the rest. Thud! The noise wakes the household, and the thief is caught!

Many historic houses have staircases with uneven risers. If the burglar-alarm staircase is a myth—and it is—what explains this?

As any good carpenter will tell you, building stairs is *hard!* In early America, stairs were built from the bottom up, one riser and tread at a time. Invariably, error crept in as more treads were installed, which meant that the final riser was probably a little taller or a little shorter than the rest. What was the carpenter supposed to do? Tear it all down and start over, or simply leave the last step a little out of whack?

Without mathematical aids, modern framing squares, and stair-building manuals of later years, it took an unusually skilled carpenter to build a stair on-site that came out exactly right. The average carpenter could build a stair that got you upstairs, but not with perfectly aligned treads and risers. Uneven risers could also have occurred during later repairs, or because the house settled over time. They were never intentional.

Myth #51

The term "hoe cake" refers to the way slaves cooked corn bread in the fields on iron hoes.

*H*oe cakes were corn bread fried in fat on griddles. The logic behind this myth is that the fields were often located far from the slave quarters, so rather than trudge back for the noon meal, it was easier to build a small fire at the edge of a field, cook some corn bread on the flat blade of a hoe, and find a piece of shade to rest and eat. It makes sense.

But the origin of the term has nothing to do with agricultural hoes. Rather, it refers to the much older meaning of "hoe," which was another word for griddle. As far back as the 1670s, when colonists baked a mixture of Indian corn on hoes (or griddles), it became known as hoe cake. The name stuck even when hoe cake was cooked in skillets or pans. Slaves cooking hoe cakes were probably cooking them over fires on griddles or in skillets. Nothing says they couldn't use flat farmers' hoes if they were griddleless, but that isn't the origin of the term.

This is one of the oldest American myths still circulating, beginning around the time of the Revolutionary War. Although several people during those years wrote about how the hoe cake got its name from the field hand's hoe, they were mistaken. The older meaning of "hoe" had been forgotten, so they found a new explanation that seemed logical.

Myth #52

Everyone was killed at the Alamo.

"Remember the Alamo!" became a famous battle cry. We may remember the Alamo, but we don't remember who died there.

The battle, in 1836, was a victory for the Mexican army under the command of General Santa Anna. His soldiers did kill all the Texans who fought against them, but they made an effort to spare many other men, women, and children in the fort. Historians argue about the exact number—was So-and-so still there, or had he left before the final fight?—but it seems that two or three African-American slaves were spared, as were the wives and children of the defenders.

The official Alamo website tries to correct the myth: "It is true that nearly all of the Texans under arms inside the fort were killed in the March 6, 1836, attack. However, nearly twenty women and children, who experienced the twelve days of siege leading to the final assault, were spared and allowed to return to their homes. The survivors also included Joe, the slave of William B. Travis. The best-known Alamo survivor, Susanna Dickinson, was sent to Gonzales by Santa Anna with a warning to the Texans that the same fate awaited them if they continued their revolt."

Myth #53

The round knob or finial at the top of a staircase
newel post is called the mortgage button and signifies
that the mortgage has been paid off.

*Y*ou'll hear it said that this is a long-standing New England
tradition, an old British custom, or a Quaker practice dating
back to the seventeenth century. Supposedly, when the mortgage
was paid off, the homeowner drilled a hole in the newel post of
the main staircase, rolled up the mortgage document, put it inside,
and capped the hole with a decorative plug. Or he burned the
document and stashed the ashes in the post.

Silly, yes, but believe it or not, there are companies that sell
"mortgage buttons" so you can install one on your own newel post
to show all your friends and relatives that you've paid off the bank
loan. Such a deal!

Trouble is, homeowner mortgages didn't exist in the
seventeenth century. Or the eighteenth. Heck, *banks* didn't exist in
the seventeenth and eighteenth centuries. Prizes have been offered
to architectural students to find proof for this popular legend, but
no one ever has. The closest anyone has come is the discovery of a
set of house plans rolled up inside a newel post in an old house.

Myth #54

People didn't bathe back then. Or: People bathed once a year. Or: Brides carried bouquets to cover up their body odor.

Well, if "bathe" means to sit in a large tub full of hot water, then yes, almost no one bathed that way until the miracle of indoor plumbing brought hot water to your tub with a turn of the wrist. But all these bathing myths imply that people didn't wash, and that is false. Just as today, personal habits varied, but most people washed at least their hands and faces daily. To bathe, they took sponge baths, usually in their bedrooms, usually standing beside their washstands with their pitchers and bowls of water, or in small tin tubs, like this one, with a few inches of warm water. Lugging buckets of water from the well, heating them on the stove, carrying them to the tub, and emptying the tub when finished was backbreaking work. Sometimes people bathed in the kitchen, nearer the stove—less privacy but less labor. Indoor showers (which originated in the mid-1800s) did not become standard in American bathrooms until the middle of the twentieth century.

One thing's for sure: People washed their hair far less often than we do today. Think how hard it was for a woman to dry her long hair without any electricity, sitting for hours by the fire or in the sun. Hairstyles reflected this reality. Until the Roaring Twenties, when women began bobbing their hair short, most women braided or twisted up their long tresses, sometimes covering them with caps. The invention of the electric hair dryer changed everything.

Accuracy might best be served by saying that although people bathed less frequently than we do today, they did not necessarily *wash* less frequently.

108 Death by Petticoat

Myth #55

Niches, called coffin corners, were built
into staircases to allow people to carry caskets
downstairs and turn a corner at the landings.

*H*ere is a myth repeated endlessly in Victorian houses with architectural niches in their staircase walls. The story goes that these niches were called coffin corners. Because most people died at home in their beds, and because most bedrooms were upstairs, it was difficult to get a casket down the stairs when the staircase turned a corner. So at the landing, a niche was cut out of the wall. By inserting one corner of the coffin into the niche, the pallbearers could make the turn at the landing. This is nonsense.

The truth? Many Victorian homes have niches built into the wall of the staircase. These were for decorative purposes, to display a statue, perhaps a bust or a vase, or maybe flowers. People usually *did* die at home, but if the bedroom was upstairs, the body could easily be carried downstairs before it was placed in a casket.

Myth #56

Some women had their lower ribs surgically removed to achieve fashionably small waists.

What started as a corset myth has morphed into current-day gossip: Have you heard that Cher had a couple ribs removed so she could retain her slender figure? Well, Cher didn't, and neither did women in Victorian America.

Not a single example of medical or historical evidence for this procedure exists. First of all, chest surgery was extremely risky. Second, anesthesia was unavailable until the middle of the 1800s and not well understood for decades afterward. Third, surgical techniques simply were not up to the task. Finding a doctor willing to undertake such a dangerous operation for cosmetic purposes was highly unlikely, and if one had ever accomplished such a feat, it would have made the medical books.

Rumors of movie stars having ribs removed probably originated with the fact that they often do have many other sorts of plastic surgery, and they often do have small waists.

Myth #57

Mirrors below tables were called petticoat mirrors, because their purpose was to allow women to make sure their petticoats weren't showing.

*T*he correct name for tables with mirrors like these are "pier tables," because they were intended for the space between two windows—that space was called a pier. Usually a mirror was fixed below the table, sometimes above it. Its purpose was both to be decorative and to reflect the light around the room, not to check petticoats. In fact, more than one experiment by costumed guides at historic houses has revealed that you cannot actually see your feet unless you stand a good distance away—and most rooms of the period were not that wide.

How did this falsehood begin? Maybe because of confusion over the words "pier" and "peer," suggesting to some that the mirror was for peering into.

Myth #58

Robert E. Lee offered to surrender his sword to Ulysses S. Grant, but Grant gallantly refused it.

*I*t's a popular myth, one heard at many Civil War battlefields and period house museums: When General Robert E. Lee surrendered at Appomattox, he offered his ceremonial sword to General U. S. Grant, who gallantly refused it.

Didn't happen. Lee never offered his sword. Grant never asked for it. The subject didn't come up. Even Grant's own words taken from his memoirs don't seem to squelch this myth. "The much talked of surrendering of Lee's sword and my handing it back," he wrote, "this and much more that has been said about it is the purest romance."

Lee's French-made sword now resides in a museum in Appomattox, Virginia, a few feet from the site of the surrender.

SURRENDER OF GENL LEE, AT APPOMATTOX C.H. VA APRIL 9TH 1865.

Myth #59

Quilt designs were really secret codes meant to assist escaping slaves through the Underground Railroad.

Since this myth surfaced in the 1990s, quilt experts, history professors, and museum curators all over the country have united to debunk it. Sadly, elementary school teachers are still teaching it to their students as fact.

The underlying premise is that quilt patterns carried messages to help slaves escape. Some claim that the quilts were maps showing escape routes. Others say quilts were made by white members of the Underground Railroad to hang outside houses to send messages. But airing quilts was routine, so how could fugitives tell which quilts were messages and which were products of good housekeeping? Still others say slaves made quilts to pass along information on the plantation. Wouldn't whispering be easier?

There is also no agreement about which patterns were used or what they meant. Rarely does a pattern have just one name—a pattern could be called Album in one region and Snowflake in another, ruining any code. Several patterns supposedly used by fugitives didn't even exist until long after slavery ended. For example, the Dresden Plate pattern (which some claim meant "Go to Dresden, Ohio") dates to the 1920s, as do the Double Wedding Ring ("Get married") and the Sunbonnet Sue ("Disguise yourself"). Why would anyone need such instructions, anyway?

There is no evidence or example of coded quilts. The Flying Geese quilt shown here is not a code for "Flee north." Firsthand accounts from former slaves and from Underground Railroad participants, black and white, tell of many ways they passed secret messages, but none mentions quilts. It's a shame that genuine stories of African-American escapes and heroism are being sidelined in favor of fanciful fiction like the Quilt Code.

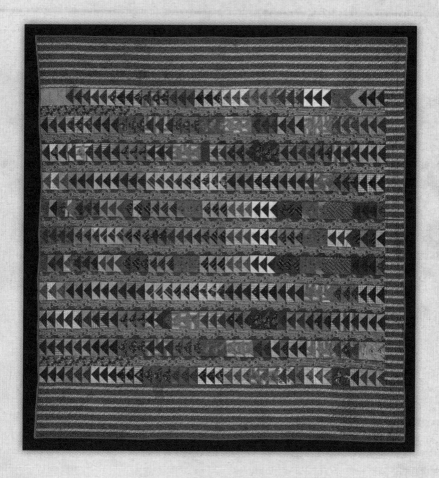

Myth #60

Quilters made mistakes on purpose
to show their humility.

*O*r: The Amish made mistakes in their quilts on purpose because "only God is perfect." Never mind that Amish quilters have denied this custom.

Quilt historians are a careful bunch, and they take unproven claims like this and the quilt code (Myth #59) very seriously. One quilt historian went looking for the origins of the "humility block" legend and found the earliest reference dated to 1949. No sources from the 1800s, such as diaries, letters, or books, mention a practice like this, and no oral tradition could be traced. Perhaps the idea got started when people noticed an odd placement of a piece of fabric or a change in color and wondered whether it had been done on purpose.

This may be an American version of the Persian-rug myth. Supposedly, the rug weaver makes a mistake on purpose because only Allah is perfect. It's not true, either. Ask any quilter, Amish or not, and he or she will tell you that plenty of mistakes are made without even trying.

Myth #61

Prudish Victorians "dressed" their naked furniture legs with fabric.

Eeeek, a naked table leg!

The idea that nineteenth-century Americans were such prudes that they covered their furniture legs with little skirts seems to have come from a satirical book written in 1839 by an Englishman about his American tour. In Frederick Marryat's *Diary in America,* he made fun of the American habit of saying "limb" instead of the more vulgar "leg." Then he visited a boarding school for young ladies in New York, and said this about a piano he saw there: "the mistress of the establishment . . . had dressed all these four limbs in modest little trousers, with frills at the bottom of them!"

Whether Marryat was exaggerating or not, he certainly was poking fun at the Americans. A search of old black-and-white photos of Victorian interiors, such as this one, failed to turn up a single example of a table, piano, or other piece of furniture with "dressed" legs. Yes, there were floor-length skirts on round tables, but heck, we do that today. Some people may have decorated with little skirts on table legs, but if so, it seems to have been rare. Those who did were indulging in the Victorians' love of lavish fabrics and excessive ornamentation, not covering up furniture legs.

Catherine Beecher, the Martha Stewart of her day, published the *American Woman's Home* in 1869 without mentioning anything about hiding naked furniture legs. Besides, what was the point of all those ornate tables with heavily carved legs if they were not meant to be seen and admired?

Myth #62

The "fainting couch" was invented during Victorian times for tightly corseted women to use when they felt faint.

What the Victorian era (technically, from 1837 to 1901) called a fainting couch was not a new invention. That flat, daybed piece of furniture has been around since ancient Egypt and Rome. But ancient Egyptians and Romans used daybeds for reclining, not to catch them as they fainted. You can see examples of antique daybeds that date from the 1600s forward in historic house museums today. In some houses, you will even hear about a "fainting room." Like the birthing-room myth (see Myth #44), this one would have us believe houses were designed with separate rooms for fainting spells. Imagine the scene: "Pardon me, sir, but I feel faint . . . would you kindly escort me to the fainting room?"

Not all Victorian-era women wore corsets, and not all laced them so tightly that they felt short of breath, but those few who did might very well have felt breathless now and then, especially during physical activity, such as dancing. Usually a brief resting spell would revive them, but on rare occasion, some did faint. And some, no doubt, faked it for dramatic value.

A daybed was a fashionable piece of furniture found in many Victorian parlors, but it was not designed or reserved for fainting women.

Myth #63

Women in early America were not allowed to use the front doors of taverns.

So they sneaked around to the back?

Women in the colonial period didn't go to taverns all that often, but there were instances when they spent nights in taverns while traveling, or dined at taverns with friends or family. Balls and lectures were occasionally held in taverns, and women certainly attended those. When colonial women entered taverns, they came through the front, side, or rear doors, whatever was most convenient.

The custom of separate ladies' entrances seems to date from the Victorian era, when some American hotels began offering ladies' entrances and ladies' waiting rooms to attract that market segment. Perhaps this myth got started when people assumed the Victorian custom had originated in colonial days.

Another myth has it that women were not allowed in bars or saloons. It is true that some Wild West saloons prohibited women from entering at all, but many bars and saloons, whether in eastern cities or frontier towns, welcomed their business, and offered separate entrances to the back rooms. This let working-class women come and go without being harassed by disapproving temperance reformers. It let them avoid wading through the rougher, all-male, stand-up barrooms with their spittoons and boisterous drunks. In the back rooms, women could socialize, buy takeout, or eat the popular free lunches—free, that is, with the purchase of a drink.

Acknowledgments

Many thanks to all the historians, curators, docents, craftsmen, and librarians who shared the myths that deviled them most, contributed their own research, and corrected me when I slipped up. I am particularly indebted to Diane Dunkley and the DAR Museum, whose 2006 exhibit Myth or Truth? Stories We've Heard About Early America inspired me to search out more history myths. A special thank-you goes to Lou Powers, Frank Clark, Susan Smyer, Nann Blaine Hilyard, Robin Kipps, Linda Baumgarten, Ed Chappell, Eric P. Olsen, Anne Dealy, Dori Cavala, Katrina Worley, Jacki Bendworth, Brett Walker, Al Saguto, Rod Cofield, Dennis Montgomery, Deborah Brower, Ron Hurst, Kenneth Schwarz, Susan Scott, Jay Gaynor, Max Hamrick, Betty Myers, Anne Dealy, Kathy Nichols, Cynthia A. Naughton, Ann Hartter, Sarah St. Germain, Becky Laudenslager, Karen Emmons, Nic Butler, Mary Jo Fairchild, Luciana Spracher, Patrick Sheary, and Alden O'Brien.

Nor could this book have been produced without encouragement and assistance from editors Paul Aron of Colonial Williamsburg and Chris Schillig of Andrews McMeel, and with help from Marianne Martin in hunting down illustrations.

Image Identifications and Credits

Unless otherwise indicated, photos in this book were taken by David M. Doody, Barbara T. Lombardi, Tom Green, and other Colonial Williamsburg photographers, and objects are from the collections of the Colonial Williamsburg Foundation.

Myth #1: Petticoat, 1770-1780. Gift of Mrs. Cora Ginsburg.

Myth #5: *Le General Washington*, by Noel Le Mire, 1775–1800

Myth #13: Painting by Sidney King. Courtesy of the Berkeley Plantation.

Myth #17: Dutch traders in New Netherland, circa 1893. Courtesy of the Library of Congress.

Myth #18: *Jamestown Massacre*, from Theodore de Bry, 1626–1627.

Myth #29: *Noon,* engraved by Richard Houston after work by Philippe Mercier, 1758.

Myth #34: "Verrerie en bois," from Denis Diderot's *Recueil de Planches . . . ,"* vol. 10.

Myth #35: Corner chair, 1740–1750. Gift of Mr. and Mrs. Leonard William Ballard, from the estate of Mary Wrenn Cofer Ballard, in honor of her daughters, Mary Wrenn Ballard Oliver and Anne Lewis Ballard Weaver.

Myth #36: Portrait of Queen Mary I, 1907. Courtesy of the Library of Congress.

Myth #37: Secretary and bookcase, William Appleton, Salem, Massachusetts, 1795–1804. Courtesy of the Winterthur Museum. Museum purchase with funds provided by Lammot du Pont Copeland.

Myth #42: *Child Holding Rattle,* attributed to Erastus Salisbury Field, circa 1838.

Myth #43: *Woman Swearing Child to a Grave Citizen*, engraved by T. Cook after a painting by William Hogarth, circa 1835 (originally published 1730–1735).

Myth #45: Statue of Major General George Brinton McClellan, Washington, DC. The George F. Landegger Collection of District of Columbia Photographs in Carol M. Highsmith's America. Courtesy of the Library of Congress.

Myth #47: Double staircase at Berry Hill Plantation, 1835 home in Halifax County, Virginia. Courtesy of the Library of Congress.

Myth #48: Pine wardrobe, Texas, 1860-1880. Courtesy of the DAR Museum. Gift of the Texas State Society.

Myth #52: *Battle of the Alamo*, by Percy Moran, 1912. Courtesy of the Library of Congress.

Myth #53: Detail of handrail at Independence Hall, Philadelphia. Courtesy of the Library of Congress.

Myth #55: Stairs at Fort Monroe, Quarters No. 1, Hampton, Virginia. Courtesy of the Library of Congress.

Myth #56: Photo of woman in corset, 1899. Courtesy of the Library of Congress.

Myth #57: Pier table, 1825–1835, attributed to Anthony Quervelle. Courtesy of the DAR Museum.

Myth #58: *Surrender of Genl. Lee at Appomattox*, by Currier and Ives, 1865. Courtesy of the Library of Congress.

Myth #59: *Flying Geese*, possibly by Deborah Middleton Parry (1830–1904). Gift of Dr. and Mrs. Paul Middleton.

Myth #60: Scripture quilt, circa 1860. Gift of George Schoellkopf.

Myth #61: Parlor, Scotia, New York, circa 1900.

Myth #62: Couch, ca. 1725.

About the Author

While Mary Miley Theobald was earning her BA and MA in American history at the College of William and Mary, she worked in costume at Colonial Williamsburg, giving tours through the historic buildings. There she learned firsthand the perils of repeating the history myths that run rampant through the museum world. She has worked for The Colonial Williamsburg Foundation in some fashion ever since—full time, part time, or on contract, writing nearly one hundred magazine articles and four books over a period of more than thirty years. Theobald also writes regularly for *Virginia Living*, and has had recent articles in *American Heritage* and the *History Channel Magazine*. She is the author of four other books, including the official bicentennial book on the Virginia Governor's Mansion. She taught museum studies and American history at Virginia Commonwealth University for thirteen years.

About The Colonial Williamsburg Foundation

The Colonial Williamsburg Foundation is a private, not-for-profit educational institution dedicated to the preservation and interpretation of the restored eighteenth-century capital of Virginia. In addition to the 301-acre Historic Area, the foundation also operates the DeWitt Wallace Decorative Arts Museum, the Abby Aldrich Rockefeller Folk Art Museum, and Bassett Hall.

Colonial Williamsburg actively supports history education in schools and homes by engaging in a wide variety of educational outreach programs and activities. These include Electronic Field Trips, which transport the story of Williamsburg and the founding of our nation to students across the country; the Colonial Williamsburg Teacher Institute, which immerses elementary, middle, and high school teachers in interdisciplinary approaches to history and government; and The Idea of America, a digital history program that covers the nation's history from its beginnings through the present, and that prepares high school students for active citizenship.

If you want to learn more about these myths or read about others, go to www.historymyths.wordpress.com.